D1317295

Published in 2013 by The Rosen Publishing Group, Inc.
29 East 21st Street, New York, NY 10010

Photo Credits: **KEY** tl=top left; tc=top center; tr=top right; cl=center left; c=center; cr=center right; bl=bottom left; bc=bottom center; br=bottom right; bg=background

ALA = Alamy; CBT = Corbis; GI = Getty Images; iS = istockphoto.com; LC = Library of Congress; TF = Topfoto; TPL = photolibrary.com

1c GI; **2–3**bg CBT; **6–7**bg iS; c TPL; **7**tc TF; **8**bl iS; **9**tl LC; **10**tr TF; **10–11**bg TF; **11**tc GI; br iS; c TF; **12**tl TF; **12–13**c TPL; **13**br, cr TF; **14**bg, bl, br, tl iS; bl, br, tl TF; **15**bg, bl iS; bl, cr, tc TF; **16–17**bg iS; bc TPL; **20**cr iS; **20–21**bg CBT; bg iS; tc TF; **21**bc, br, c, cr iS; bl, br, tl, tr TF; **22–23**bg, tr CBT; **24**tl CBT; bl iS; bl TF; **24–25**bc CBT; bg, bg iS; **25**tc LC; br TF; **26**bl TF; **26–27**bg iS; tc LC; **27**cr ALA; tr iS; bl iS; br TF; **28–29**bg iS; cl TF; **29**br CBT; bc GI; c, c, cl, cr, tl, tr TF; **30**bc, cr, tr TF; c TPL; **30–31**bg iS; **31**bg TPL; **32**bg TP

All illustrations copyright Weldon Owen Pty Ltd. **16**tl Andrew Davies/Creative Communication

Weldon Owen Pty Ltd
Managing Director: Kay Scarlett
Creative Director: Sue Burk
Publisher: Helen Bateman
Senior Vice President, International Sales: Stuart Laurence
Vice President Sales North America: Ellen Towell
Administration Manager, International Sales: Kristine Ravn

Library of Congress Cataloging-in-Publication Data

Park, Louise, 1961–
The sinking of the Titanic / by Louise Park.
    p. cm. — (Discovery education: sensational true stories)
Includes index.
ISBN 978-1-4777-0057-0 (library binding) — ISBN 978-1-4777-0099-0 (pbk.) —
ISBN 978-1-4777-0100-3 (6-pack)
1. Titanic (Steamship)—Juvenile literature. 2. Shipwrecks—North Atlantic Ocean—Juvenile literature. I. Title.
G530.T6P35 2013
910.9163'4—dc23
                    2012019576

Manufactured in the United States of America

CPSIA Compliance Information: Batch #W13PK2: For Further Information contact Rosen Publishing, New York, New York at 1-800-237-9932

SENSATIONAL TRUE STORIES

THE SINKING OF THE TITANIC

LOUISE PARK

PowerKiDS press.

New York

Contents

A Disaster Story

The *Titanic* was an ocean liner which, for its time, was the largest and most luxurious passenger steamship in the world. It was built between 1909 and 1912. It was designed by some of the most experienced engineers of the day and used the latest technology. On April 10, 1912, it set sail on its maiden voyage—its very first voyage—from Southampton, England, to New York. There were 2,223 people on board. Four days into the voyage, shortly before midnight on April 14, the *Titanic* struck an iceberg. It took two hours and forty minutes for the ship to sink. More than 1,500 lives were lost.

The investigations after the tragic sinking brought about important changes to maritime law across the world.

In the news
The sinking of the *Titanic* came as a great shock to the public because so much had been made of its use of advanced technology and all its safety features. The newspapers reported stories about the disaster for a very long time.

An unsinkable ship?
The *Titanic*'s owners, the White Star Line, never stated that the ship was unsinkable. This claim was not made until after the ship actually sank. The first claim that the *Titanic* was unsinkable appeared the day after the disaster, in the *New York Times*.

Design and Construction

S hipbuilding was a big and competitive business in the early 1900s. With no airplanes, people who needed to travel long distances had to go by sea. Big shipping companies, such as the White Star Line, which owned the *Titanic,* competed for customers by providing comfortable, safe, fast transport. The *Titanic* had two steam engines and one low-pressure turbine that drove three propellers. Its top speed was 24 knots, or 26 miles per hour (43 km/h).

Ship details

The *Titanic* was 882 feet (270 m) long and 175 feet (53 m) high from the keel to the top of its funnels. The hull was designed to be watertight. If one hull section flooded, the water was supposed to remain contained within that hull section. It would not flood out into other sections.

The *Titanic* was built in Belfast, Ireland.

SIZE COMPARISONS

The *Titanic* was almost four times longer than today's Airbus A380 airplane. It was about three-quarters the length of the largest cruise ship operating in the world today, the *Oasis of the Seas,* a luxury liner that is 1,187 feet (363 m) long.

Airbus A380   RMS *Titanic*   *Oasis of the Seas*

Steel hull
The hull was made of steel plates held together by millions of rivets.

Bulkhead
The bulkheads were steel walls that separated the hull into 16 sections.

The shipyard
The *Titanic* was built at Harland and Wolff shipyard in Belfast, Ireland. Work began on March 31, 1909, and it took more than 3,000 workers three years to construct it and fit out the interiors.

First-class staterooms
These passengers were rich, even famous, international travelers on business or vacation.

Third-class cabins
The 262 cabins were paneled with pine and were much better than third-class cabins on other ships

First-class dining room
As many as 532 people could dine in this huge, elegant room.

Third-class dining room
It was located on F deck, and the decor was bright and comfortable.

Main galley
The main kitchen was enormous. It prepared the meals for first and second class.

Steam engines
The two engines were powered by 29 boilers fired by 159 coal furnaces.

Second-class cabins
Each of the 162 cabins had a washbasin and two or four berths built into the walls with curtains for a little privacy.

Second-class dining room
The oak-paneled room was so large it seated 400 second-class guests.

Third-class kitchen
A typical dinner was rice soup, corned beef with cabbage and potatoes, then peaches and rice.

Did You Know?
Passengers in first class, second class, and third class were in separate areas. The first-class section was located mostly on or above the boat deck level, so it was closer to the lifeboats.

Berths

The *Titanic* could carry 3,547 passengers and crew. On its maiden voyage, it sailed with more than 2,200 people, who slept in first class, second class, third class, and also the crews' quarters. First class had an elite section of 39 private suites. Each suite had up to five rooms and its own promenade. First class also had 350 cheaper cabins, each with a single bed. Second class had two-berth or four-berth cabins. In third class, also known as steerage, passengers slept in two-berth to six-berth cabins. There were open berthing sections, too.

Stateroom
The paneled staterooms were luxuriously furnished with a table, chair, basins with hot and cold running water, and a bed.

Cost of a ticket

Originally purchased in British currency, a first-class suite today would cost the equivalent of $50,000! A first-class cabin would cost around $1,724, and second-class accommodations around $690. A third-class ticket cost the equivalent of between $172 and $460 in today's dollars. All meals were included in the ticket price.

Private suite
The best accommodation was a private suite in first class. Private suites had a bedroom with a curtained bed, a sitting room, a bathroom, a wardrobe room, and a servants' room.

KEY
- ☐ First class
- ▨ Second class
- ■ Third class

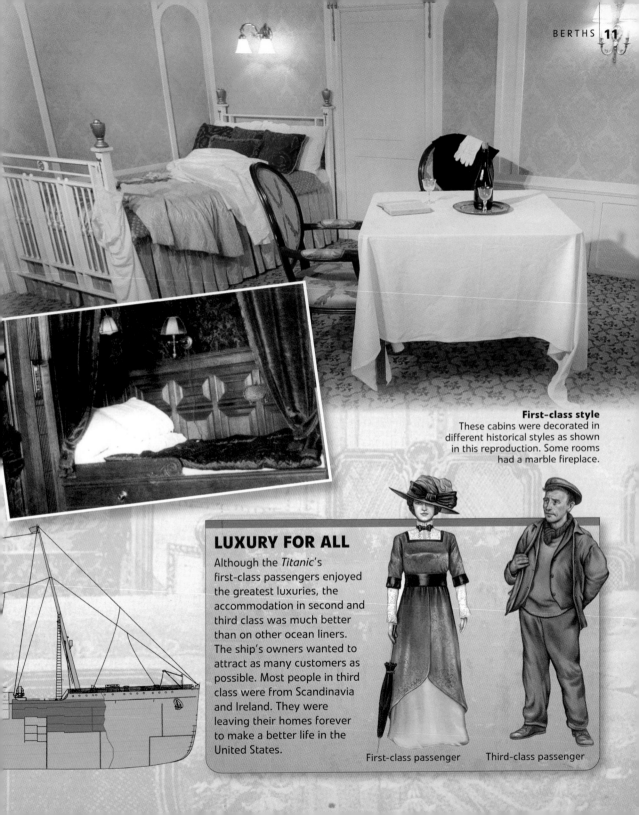

First-class style
These cabins were decorated in different historical styles as shown in this reproduction. Some rooms had a marble fireplace.

LUXURY FOR ALL

Although the *Titanic*'s first-class passengers enjoyed the greatest luxuries, the accommodation in second and third class was much better than on other ocean liners. The ship's owners wanted to attract as many customers as possible. Most people in third class were from Scandinavia and Ireland. They were leaving their homes forever to make a better life in the United States.

First-class passenger

Third-class passenger

Boat deck
There were separate areas where first-class and second-class passengers and officers could stroll. Most of the lifeboats were stowed there, too.

Life On Board

The *Titanic* offered more facilities than any other luxury ocean liner. Both first class and second class had libraries and barbershops. Third-class passengers had a large general room where they could meet. The steam-powered generators provided electricity and electric lighting throughout the ship, as well as four electric elevators. Two Marconi radios were available for sending telegraphs. The ship had a hospital and its own newspaper, printed daily.

Luxury facilities

First-class passengers could exercise in the heated swimming pool, gymnasium, and squash court, and enjoy the Turkish baths or an electrically heated bath. They could eat at the dining saloon or the Café Parisien, which was modeled on a sidewalk café in Paris and served superior food.

The gymnasium
First-class passengers could use an electric camel, an electric horse, stationary bicycles, and a rowing machine at the gymnasium.

The Grand Staircase

First-class passengers entered the *Titanic* via the Grand Staircase. It descended five levels down to E deck, and the stairwell reached more than 60 feet (18 m) to the glass skylight above. On each landing, a bronze cherub held a lamp. The balustrades were gilded. The entire staircase was paneled in polished oak.

The Turkish baths
The Turkish baths were located behind the swimming pool. They had a steam room, a hot room, a temperature room, shampooing rooms, a toilet, and a cooling-off room.

The Crew

Captain Edward J. Smith
This experienced English naval officer
was 62 years old. The *Titanic*'s maiden
voyage was to be his last before he
retired. His body was never recovered.

The crew of the *Titanic* totaled 899 men
and women, under the command of
Captain Edward J. Smith. The deck
crew consisted of a master-at-arms,
officers, store masters, and seamen, who
were responsible for sailing and navigating.
The engineering department consisted of
electricians, firemen, boilermen, and
engineers. They kept the engines running
and the ship going. Then there were the
stewards and kitchen staff, restaurant staff,
musicians, and post staff, who looked after
the passengers.

First Officer William Murdoch
He was on the bridge when the ship
hit the iceberg and gave the order to
turn the ship. He loaded passengers
into lifeboats but did not survive.

Wireless operator Jack Phillips
Jack Phillips sent out the distress
signal after the collision. He stayed at
his post until the wireless room filled
with water. He did not survive.

The *Titanic*'s officers
Four of the *Titanic*'s eight officers, who are pictured here, died along with their captain (center right). Only 215 of the 899 crew survived the sinking of the *Titanic*.

Wallace Henry Hartley

THE BANDMASTER

There were two bands on board. Led by the bandmaster, Wallace Henry Hartley, they played together on the boat deck after the collision to calm the passengers. Survivors claim the band played to the very end. None of them survived.

Wireless operator Harold Bride
The junior wireless operator made contact with the *Carpathia*, the rescue ship. He was at his post until the wireless room flooded, but managed to survive.

ICEBERG ALLEY

Iceberg Alley is a notorious stretch of water, full of icebergs and sea ice, about 250 miles (400 km) east and southeast of Newfoundland, Canada. An iceberg floating south from this area collided with the ship. There were 1,019 icebergs reported in the transatlantic shipping lane in the iceberg season of 1912. Most were sighted in April.

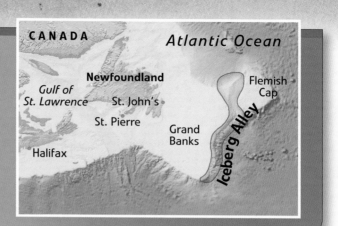

CANADA

Atlantic Ocean

Newfoundland

Gulf of St. Lawrence

St. John's

St. Pierre

Grand Banks

Halifax

Flemish Cap

Iceberg Alley

NORTH AMERICA

3. Iceberg
At 11:40 p.m. on April 14, the ship was about 400 miles (645 km) south of Newfoundland's Grand Banks when the two lookouts spotted a large iceberg.

NEW YORK

ATLANTIC OCEAN

Setting Out

The *Titanic* was built to sail the popular transatlantic travel route from England to North America, which took about six days to complete. The ship began its voyage on April 10, 1912, from Southampton, England, with some of the most prominent people of the day on board, traveling in first class. As the *Titanic* left its berth, its wake caused another ocean liner, the SS *New York*, to break from its mooring. The two ships drew dangerously close and almost collided.

The first sighting

Lookout Frederick Fleet was on duty in the crow's nest and saw the iceberg only when it was directly in front of the ship. He sounded the ship's bell three times. Then, he telephoned the bridge and shouted into the phone, "Iceberg, right ahead!" First Officer Murdoch immediately gave the order to turn the ship.

2. Queenstown (Cork)
It went on to Queenstown, in Ireland, where it took on more passengers, many of whom were Irish people emigrating to the United States.

SOUTHAMPTON

QUEENSTOWN (CORK)

CHERBOURG

1. Cherbourg
The ship crossed the English Channel and stopped at Cherbourg, in France. Some passengers got off, while others boarded the ship.

EUROPE

AFRICA

Heading for the Atlantic

Once the *Titanic* was clear of the Irish coast, it made good progress across the Atlantic. There were some reports that the captain had been encouraged to sail fast in an attempt to beat the record for an Atlantic crossing.

Collision!

After hearing the warning, the crew began to turn the ship, but it was too late. As "Stop" lit up the indicator board in the boiler rooms, a massive rumble was heard. Icy-cold water blasted through the forward boiler rooms. The *Titanic* had been hit by an iceberg about 450 miles (725 km) from New York. The ice mass had brushed the right side of the ship and buckled the hull in several places. About 299 feet (90 m) of thick steel sheets had been smashed in along the ship's side.

"*Iceberg, right ahead!*"

FREDERICK FLEET, LOOKOUT IN THE CROW'S NEST OF THE *TITANIC*, 11:40 P.M., APRIL 14, 1912

Water

Watertight compartments
The ship could stay afloat if up to four of its sixteen watertight compartments were flooded. But the first five compartments had been breached by the collision and started taking on water.

Hidden below
Typically, about only one tenth of an iceberg sits above the surface of the water. The other nine tenths are hidden below the surface. This makes icebergs very difficult to see. The *Titanic* had heard several radio warnings that there were icebergs in the area, and had changed its course. However, when the lookout saw the iceberg ahead, the ship was going too fast to stop or turn in time.

Two hours left

Alerted by the crash, Captain Smith went onto the bridge and ordered a complete stop. He ordered an officer to make a tour of the forward area and report back quickly. The officer did this with one of the ship's designers and returned to tell the captain that the *Titanic* would stay afloat for about two hours. Soon after midnight, the captain ordered that the lifeboats be made ready.

The Lifeboats

The *Titanic* carried 20 lifeboats. Lifeboats 1–16 were wooden and could take 40 or 65 people each. Lifeboats A, B, C, and D were collapsible and could hold 47 people each. The *Titanic* had enough lifeboats to rescue 1,178 people—about 53 percent of everyone on board. The first lifeboat was launched at 12:45 a.m. with only 28 people. By 1:30 a.m., almost all of the lifeboats had been launched, leaving most of the passengers and crew on board.

1. Lining up
First-class and second-class passengers lined up to board the lifeboats. Many passengers in third class could not find their way from the lower decks to reach the lifeboat deck in time.

Wooden lifeboats

The *Titanic* had space for 64 wooden lifeboats on its deck, which would have held more than 4,000 people. The law at that time required that a ship such as the *Titanic* should have 16 wooden lifeboats.

2. Loading the boats
Officers helped to load women and children into the lifeboats. The rule for loading lifeboats was: women and children first. As a result, more men died in the disaster than women.

3. Being lowered
Many lifeboats were less than half full when they were lowered to the water. The first two lifeboats launched with only 28 people each. From the boat deck to the waterline was 59 feet (18 m).

4. Getting away
A total of 18 lifeboats were launched before the *Titanic* sank. When people saw it would go down, they scrambled to get on the last few lifeboats. Some men were allowed on to work the oars.

5. Returning to save others
Once the *Titanic* went down, it was safe for the lifeboats to return to the area to pick up people in the water. However, only two lifeboats did this because the people were afraid.

Breaking Up

As the *Titanic*'s bow filled with water, it started to sink. At about 1:40 a.m., freezing water flooded onto the bow. Ten minutes later, the forward well decks were underwater and the promenade of the forward A deck was perilously close to the waterline. By about 2:05 a.m., water was up around the bridge railing. As the stern rose out of the water, the propellers were exposed and the *Titanic* tilted ever more steeply. By 2:10 a.m., 18 of the 20 lifeboats had been launched, but about 1,500 people were still on board.

THE SINKING

In the first hour after being hit, it was not obvious that the ship was going down. Passengers did not believe the *Titanic* would sink and were reluctant to leave a big, safe ship for a little wooden lifeboat.

The final moments

At 2:17 a.m., the last call for help was sent out from the *Titanic*'s radio room. As the stern rose higher in the air, anything not bolted down crashed toward the water. The forward funnel collapsed and crushed some people. Others jumped overboard in the hope of reaching a lifeboat. At about 2:20 a.m., the ship's lights went out. Then, the bow broke away from the stern.

1 Taking on water
Water enters the rip along the hull. The first five hull compartments start taking on water.

2 Bow going down
The weight in the bow makes it sink below the waterline. The stern rises up out of the water.

3 Hull breaking apart
At 2.20 a.m., the hull breaks in two between the rear two funnels. The bow sinks.

4 In two pieces
The stern rights itself and floats briefly, until it fills with water and goes under, too.

Did You Know?

When the ship broke in two, the bow sank but the ship's stern settled back on the water and became level for a moment. Then it slowly filled with water, rose up, and sank as well.

The Rescue

From 12:15 a.m. onward, the *Titanic*'s radio operators sent out distress signals. At 12:32 a.m., the *Carpathia* answered: "Putting about and heading for you." It went as fast as it could, but took more than three hours to reach the area. By then, some passengers had been in the lifeboats for more than three hours and had died from hypothermia. The *Carpathia* managed to rescue about 705 people.

The *Carpathia*'s radio room
David Sarnoff picked up the *Titanic*'s distress signals in the radio room of the *Carpathia* at 12:32 a.m.

Commemorative medal
Arthur Henry Rostron, the captain of the *Carpathia*, was awarded this medal for his heroic work during the rescue effort.

RECOGNITION

The *Carpathia* was 58 miles (93 km) away from the *Titanic* when it received the distress call from the sinking ship. The *Carpathia*'s crew worked hard to pick up the people in the lifeboats and bring them aboard the rescue vessel. The survivors were given dry clothing, warm blankets, food, and drink, and a short prayer service was held for them and for those who had died. Later, the survivors awarded medals to the crew of the *Carpathia* for their rescue work.

Crew of the *Carpathia*

FOR HEROICALLY SAVING THE SEVEN HUNDRED A... TITANIC IN MID... THE THANKS OF CONGRESS · TO ARTHUR H...

Waiting for survivors
The *Carpathia* left the rescue area at about
8:50 a.m. on April 15 and docked in New
York that evening. Crowds had gathered
to watch the rescue ship come in and to
welcome the *Titanic*'s survivors.

The New York Times.

"All the News That's
Fit to Print."

ONE CENT

NEW YORK, TUESDAY, APRIL 16, 1912—TWENTY-FOUR PAGES.

TITANIC SINKS FOUR HOURS AFTER HITTING ICEBERG;
866 RESCUED BY CARPATHIA, PROBABLY 1250 PERISH;
ISMAY SAFE, MRS. ASTOR MAYBE, NOTED NAMES MISSING

Biggest Liner Plunges
to the Bottom
at 2:20 A.M.

RESCUERS THERE TOO LATE

Except to Pick Up the Few Hun-
dreds Who Took to the
Lifeboats.

WOMEN AND CHILDREN FIRST

Cunarder Carpathia Rushing to
New York with the
Survivors.

SEA SEARCH FOR OTHERS

The California Stands By on
Chance of Picking Up Other
Boats or Rafts.

OLYMPIC SENDS THE NEWS

The Lost Titanic Being Towed Out of Belfast Harbor.

PARTIAL LIST OF THE SAVED.

Headline news
Unconfirmed
reports of the
disaster were
front-page news
the day after the
Titanic sank.

Lessons Learned

After the *Titanic* sank, many people investigated the reasons for the disaster. Because of this, governments and shipping companies made many changes to prevent such an accident from happening again. The transatlantic shipping lanes were moved farther south, away from Iceberg Alley. The International Ice Patrol was established to monitor icebergs and warn ships about the location of icebergs.

NEW SAFETY REGULATIONS

The first International Convention for the Safety of Life at Sea was held in 1913. It created a set of rules that all ships had to follow. Some rules were: ships must conduct lifeboat training and lifeboat drills during each voyage; ships must provide a lifeboat space for every person on board; ships must maintain a 24-hour radio watch so they can pick up distress signals from other ships.

All that remained of the *Titanic* afterward were the lifeboats.

Senate inquiry
The US Senate Investigating Committee questioned people in New York after the disaster.

Did You Know?

The *Titanic* sailed with 2,223 people on board. It had the capacity to carry 3,547 people. If it had sailed with its full load, many more lives would have been lost.

Tragedy or Curse?
Many people believed
that the *Titanic* was
cursed. The White Star
Line did not christen
their ships, which was
the usual custom, and
superstitious people
felt this was a mistake.
Some people also thought
that the sinking fulfilled
a prophecy in a novel
about a ship called
Titan that was written
years before.

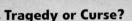

CURIOUS FACTS

Two dogs were rescued from
the sinking ship.

Only three of the *Titanic*'s
four funnels actually functioned.
The fourth was just to make the
ship looked more spectacular.

Cats were often brought on board
ships for good luck, but the *Titanic*
sailed with none.

Rediscovery

The wreck of the *Titanic* lay on the ocean floor for 73 years before it was discovered. In 1985, Robert Ballard and Jean-Louis Michel conducted an expedition. They found the hull 2.3 miles (3.7 km) below the surface, 370 miles (595 km) southeast of Mistaken Point, in Newfoundland. The stern section was found 1,970 feet (600 m) away from the bow and facing in the opposite direction.

Treasures from beneath the sea

The ocean floor in the area around the bow and stern of the *Titanic* was covered with broken bits of ship, pieces of furniture, dinnerware, and personal items. Archaeologists recovered more than 6,000 artifacts from the ship's grave. These included clothing, personal letters, banknotes, jewelry, porcelain, and even picture frames.

The bell
This bell from the *Titanic* is now on exhibition in a maritime museum.

Basin
This basin came from a first-class berth. There are faucets for hot and cold water.

Porthole
Several portholes were brought to the surface and kept.

Crockery
A surprising number of dinner plates, cups, and saucers were unbroken.

Gold jewelry
A necklace with a gold nugget was among the jewelry that was brought to the surface.

Binoculars
A pair of binoculars was among the many personal possessions found.

Travel Brochure

Prior to the *Titanic*'s maiden voyage the White Star Line did extensive advertising to attract passengers.

Create your own travel brochure for the *Titanic*.

1 Examine existing travel brochures from travel agencies and Internet sites about ocean liners for ideas. Remember that your brochure needs to reflect the era of 1912.

2 Consider your intended audience. Will you target the wealthy of 1912? If so, how will you do it? What language might you use to appeal to this group of the population at this time?

3 Consider what key information your potential passengers will want to know and revisit this book for ideas. Some important things to include are information on price, safety, the ship's intended journey, and the length of time it will take to complete it.

4 Make a list of all the features and facilities onboard the *Titanic* that you think would attract customers and decide how you will present it in your brochure.

5 Decide which images you will include to best advertise the ship's strengths.

6 Design and construct your brochure.

Glossary

archaeologists
(ahr-kee-AH-luh-jist)
People who study
human history by
excavating sites
and examining
remaining artifacts.

balustrade
(BA-luh-strayd) A row of
railings next to stairs.

bow (BOW) The forward
part of the hull of a ship.

breached (BREECHD)
Broken open.

christen (KRIS-en)
To name or dedicate
a vessel with a ceremony
and bottle of champagne
that is broken against
the ship.

crow's nest
(KROHZ NEST) A platform
fixed at the top of a mast
of a vessel and used as
a lookout.

cursed (KURSD)
Inflicted with a
supernatural power
that causes harm.

hull (HUL) The main
body of a ship that
includes the bottom,
sides, and deck but
not the mast, riggings,
and engines.

hypothermia
(hy-puh-THUR-mee-uh)
A dangerously low
body temperature.

keel (KEEL) A structure
that provides structural
strength to the ship.
The keel sits underneath
the ship in the center
and runs the length of
the ship.

maritime law
(MAR-ih-tym LAW)
A body of law that
governs maritime issues,
offenses, and incidents.

mooring (MOOR-ing)
A place where a vessel
is secured.

porcelain (POR-suh-lin)
White ceramic china.

promenade
(prah-mih-NAYD)
A walkway.

prophecy
(PRAH-feh-see)
A prediction that
something will happen
in the future.

rivets (RIH-vetz)
Metal pins or bolts used
to hold two pieces of
metal together.

stern (STERN) The rear
part of the ship.

wake (WAYK)
Waves made by a
moving vessel.

Index

B
bow 22, 23, 28, 29

C
Carpathia 15, 24, 25

F
facilities 12, 13, 30
first class 9, 10, 11, 12, 13, 16, 20, 29

H
hull 8, 18, 23, 28

I
International Convention for the Safety of Life at
   Sea 26
International Ice Patrol 26

S
second class 9, 10, 11, 12, 20
stern 22, 23, 28, 29

T
third class 9, 10, 11, 12, 20
transatlantic shipping lanes 16, 26
travel route 16, 17

U
US Senate Investigating Committee 26

W
watertight compartments 8, 18, 23
White Star Line 7, 8, 27, 30

Websites

Due to the changing nature of Internet links, PowerKids Press has developed an online list of websites related to the subject of this book. This site is updated regularly. Please use this link to access the list: www.powerkidslinks.com/disc/titan/

28 DAY LOAN

Hewlett-Woodmere Public Library
Hewlett, New York 11557-0903

Business Phone 516-374-1967
Recorded Announcements 516-374-1667